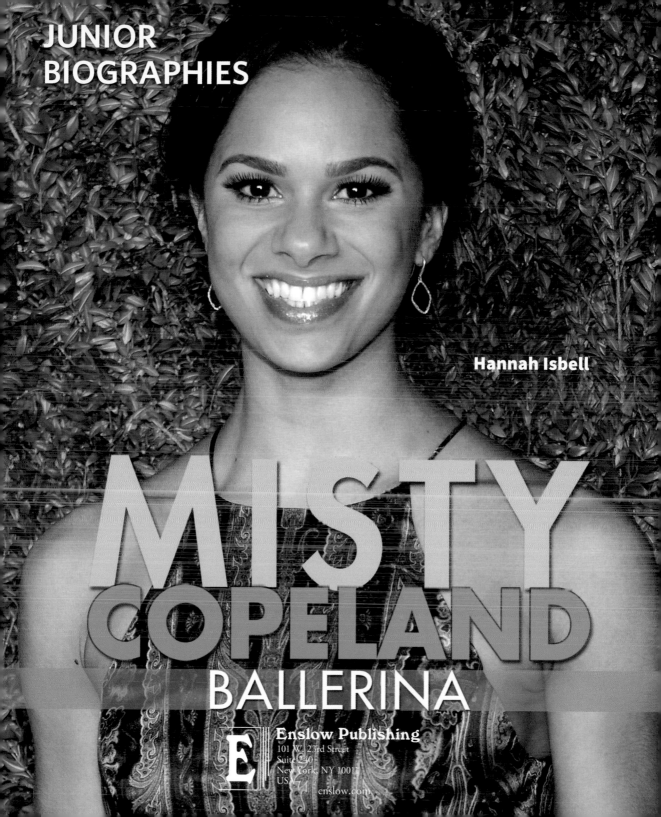

JUNIOR
BIOGRAPHIES

Hannah Isbell

MISTY
COPELAND
BALLERINA

Enslow Publishing
101 W. 23rd Street
Suite 240
New York, NY 10011
USA

enslow.com

WORDS TO KNOW

autobiography A book written by a person about his or her own life.

ballet A classical form of dance.

barre The warm-up practiced in a ballet class at a hand railing.

choreograph To come up with the steps and movements of a dance routine.

diversity Having multiple types of something.

mentor A trusted and experienced adviser and teacher.

pinnacle The top.

principal The main dancer in a company.

prodigy A young person with exceptional talent.

soloist The only artist on a stage.

stereotypes Ideas of a person that are widely held but not necessarily accurate.

CONTENTS

CHAPTER 1

BREAKING BARRIERS

In 2015 Misty Copeland made headlines when she was named the **principal** ballerina of the American Ballet Theatre. Misty is the first African American woman to earn the title of top dancer in the ballet company's history. Misty is a world-famous athlete. President Barack Obama made her a member of the President's Council on Fitness, Sports, and Nutrition in 2014. She's danced all over the country, on Broadway, and on TV. She worked hard to be a dancer, and she broke many barriers to do it.

FINDING DANCE

Misty was born on September 10, 1982, in Kansas City, Missouri, but moved to California when she was very

Misty Says:
"My first ballet class was on a basketball court. I'm in my gym clothes and my socks, trying to do this thing called ballet, and I didn't know anything about it. Once I was a part of it, I couldn't get enough of it."

young. Her family didn't have very much money and they moved often. After separating from her father, Misty's mother moved Misty and her five brothers and sisters into a motel. At twelve years old, Misty had to share two rooms with her siblings and mother.

Misty and her family lived in a motel when she was young. Ballet became a way for her to escape the motel and focus on something positive.

Misty had always loved to dance and would **choreograph** her own steps to pop songs. She was captain of her school's drill team and used her choreography for their routines. Misty's coach noticed her natural grace. When Misty was thirteen, her coach suggested she try **ballet**.

Fun Fact

Even though ballet was first created over 500 years ago, women weren't allowed to dance ballet until 1681.

There were free ballet classes at the local Boys and Girls Club. At first, Misty just watched the classes, not sure if she wanted to join in. When she decided to give it a try, she found she loved it! Soon, she was going to classes every week and using the railing of the motel balcony as a practice **barre**. Misty didn't like living at the motel, and she called practice an "escape."

Ballet created a rift between Misty's teacher and her mother. Considered a prodigy, Misty was expected to practice long hours.

CHAPTER 2
MOVING ON UP

Misty's talent made her stand out from the start. It takes most ballerinas three years to get up on their toes, but Misty was *en pointe* in only three months! Her ballet teacher, Cindy Bradley, said she could master any step she was shown. She was considered a **prodigy**. But Misty stood out for other reasons, too.

Misty comes from a mixed family. Her father, Doug Copeland, is German American and African American, and her mother, Sylvia DelaCerna, is Italian American and African American. There is not a lot of **diversity** in ballet. Misty stood out as a person of color, and as a person from a poor family.

Being *en pointe* is difficult and requires a lot of strength. *En pointe* is a signature style of ballet and is very important to the dance.

FUN FACT

The Nutcracker is performed nearly 1,000 times every year in the United States!

A RISING STAR

Misty's living situation made it hard for her to keep up with ballet. Soon, her ballet teacher offered to host her. Misty moved in with her ballet teacher's family so she could spend more time studying dance. On weekends, she would take a two-hour bus ride to visit her family.

During this time, Misty won several competitions and awards. People began to notice her. She caught the media's attention when she performed as Clara in *The Nutcracker* after only eight months of studying ballet. Every performance, 2,000 people would show up to watch her!

When she was 16, she won a scholarship to the American Ballet Theatre's (ABT) summer program in New York City.

ON HER OWN

When Misty finished high school, she moved to New York City to join the ABT. In 2001, she became a member of their corps de ballet. As the only black woman in the corps, she felt a lot of pressure.

At first, the pressure of being one of the few people of color in ballet was hard for Misty to handle. She had to fight many **stereotypes**. There was some racism in ballet's

The "Dance of the Sugarplum Fairy" is one of the most famous scenes in *The Nutcracker*.

Craig Salstein and Misty Copeland perform *Giselle* in 2015.

history. Black people were told they didn't belong.

Misty began to doubt herself. She became self-conscious about her body and about being different. Soon, her dancing began to suffer.

Misty Says:
"To me, I look like a ballerina, and I feel like a ballerina."

When she was 19, her teachers and coaches at the ABT noticed her struggles. Susan Fales-Hill, one of the members of the board of directors, decided to be her mentor. She introduced Misty to many black women trailblazers. These women helped Misty regain her confidence. Soon, she was dancing in top form once more.

Meeting other strong black women also helped Misty see that being an African American ballerina gave her a special opportunity: she could be a role model and show kids how to fight stereotypes and break barriers. President Obama said that she is "somebody who has entered a field that's very competitive… and through sheer force of will and determination, and incredible talent and hard work, she was able to arrive at the pinnacle of her field."

In 2004, she had a breakthrough season. Every show she danced in was a success. Misty was made a soloist in

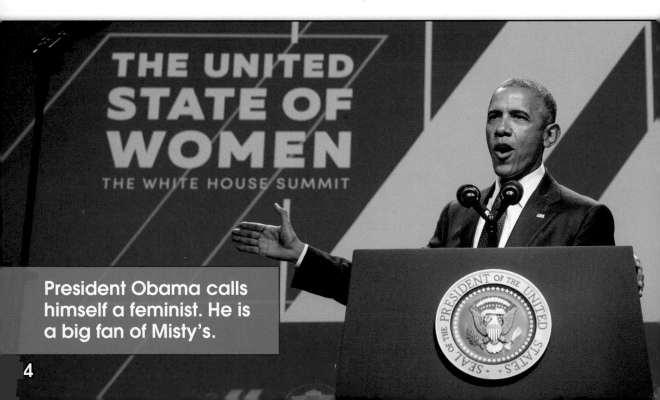

President Obama calls himself a feminist. He is a big fan of Misty's.

2010, and in 2012 she starred in *Firebird,* her first major lead. As she achieved more starring roles and recognition, she used her place in the spotlight to promote diversity in ballet. She worked especially hard to encourage kids of all backgrounds to dance. She even cowrote a book for kids about ballet and titled it *Firebird* after her first major role.

It is important to Misty that she encourages the next generation of dancers.

FUN FACT

Pointe shoes are usually only worn for one performance. They wear out after intense dancing!

15

Swan Lake is another famous ballet. Misty was able to dance the lead in 2015.

Misty is a strong spokesperson for people of color. Through her talent and hard work, she leapt to worldwide fame. Now she is working to make the world more inclusive and accepting of everyone, no matter what color skin or type of body they have.

Misty Says:

"I didn't want to pancake my skin to be a lighter color. I didn't want to wear make up to make my nose look thinner. I wanted to be myself."

CHAPTER 4
MORE ON THE HORIZON

Misty has already broken many barriers as the first woman of color solo ballerina. But that is not enough for her. In 2011, she released her own line of dancewear, M by Misty, which was designed to be worn by girls that didn't have the typical ballerina body type. She danced with famed musician Prince and served as a guest judge on the 11th season of FOX's *So You Think You Can Dance?* in 2013.

The more famous she became, the more in demand she was. She has been in commercials for American Express, COACH, Diet Dr. Pepper, and most recently, UnderArmour. Her campaigns for UnderArmour are some of the most popular and successful in the brand's history, and the company credits Misty with a huge jump in sales.

Misty Says:

"They're being told they won't fit in, they won't have a successful career, they don't have the bodies. Even to this day I hear that I shouldn't be wearing a tutu. That I don't have the right legs, my muscles are too big."

Prince recognized Misty's talent and performed with her many times.

In 2014, Misty released an **autobiography**, *Life in Motion*, which immediately became a *New York Times* best seller. That same year, she received an honorary doctorate from the University of Hartford.

Personally, Misty is very proud of her ability to inspire young girls. In 2016, Misty was made into a Barbie, introducing her to a new group of children around the world. She works very hard to be an inspiration to others. She is engaged to be married to attorney Olu Evans and lives in New York City.

Misty has spent her life working very hard to change the way the world sees ballet and dancers.

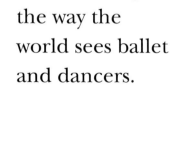

Misty and her Barbie in 2016.

Over her career, she has focused on proving that through hard work and determination anything is possible. The future looks bright for Misty Copeland, her career, and the world of dance.

Misty is an internationally recognized talent. She has broken many barriers in the world of dance.

TIMELINE

1982 Misty Copeland is born in Kansas City, Missouri

1996 Attends her first ballet class at the Boys and Girls Club

1999 Begins performing with the American Ballet Theatre

2001 Becomes a member of the corps de ballet

2004 Misty's breakthrough season

2007 Appointed soloist

2012 Starred in the critically acclaimed performance of *Firebird*

2014 Published a children's book, *Firebird*, and autobiography, *Life in Motion*

2014 Named to the President's Council on Fitness, Sports, and Nutrition; receives honorary doctorate

2015 Appointed principal dancer of the American Ballet Theatre

2016 Is made into a Barbie

LEARN MORE

BOOKS

Allen, Debbie. *Dancing in the Wings.* New York, NY: Penguin, 2003.

Calkhoven, Laurie, and Patricia Castalao. *Women Who Changed the World.* New York, NY: Scholastic, 2016.

Copeland, Misty, and Christopher Myers. *Firebird.* New York, NY: Penguin, 2014.

WEBSITES

American Ballet Theatre

www.abt.org

The American Ballet Theatre's official website. See all the dancers and shows of the company.

Fitness

www.fitness.gov

The President's Council on Fitness, Sports, and Nutrition.

Misty Copeland

www.mistycopeland.com

Misty Copeland's official website, where you can read more about her, watch videos, and catch up on her latest work.

INDEX

Published in 2017 by Enslow Publishing, LLC.
101 W. 23rd Street, Suite 240, New York, NY 10011

Copyright © 2017 by Enslow Publishing, LLC.

Library of Congress Cataloging-in-Publication Data

Names: Isbell, Hannah, author.
Title: Misty Copeland : ballerina / Hannah Isbell.
Description: New York, NY : Enslow Publishing, 2017. | Series: Junior biographies
| Includes bibliographical references and index.
Identifiers: LCCN 2016020287| ISBN 9780766081796 (library bound) | ISBN
9780766081772 (pbk.) | ISBN 9780766081789 (6-pack)
Subjects: LCSH: Copeland, Misty—Juvenile literature. | Ballet dancers—United
States—Biography—Juvenile literature. | African American dancers—Biography—
Juvenile literature.
Classification: LCC GV1785.C635 I74 2016 | DDC 792.802/8092 [B]—dc23
LC record available at https://lccn.loc.gov/2016020287

Printed in China

To Our Readers: We have done our best to make sure all websites in this book were active and appropriate when we went to press. However, the author and the publisher have no control over and assume no liability for the material available on those websites or on any websites they may link to. Any comments or suggestions can be sent by email to customerservice@enslow.com.

Photo Credits: Cover, p. 1 Andrew Toth/Getty Images; p. 4 Brad Barket/BET/Getty Images; p. 6 (top) James R. Martin/Shutterstock.com; p. 7 © AP Images; p. 9 CBS Photo Archive/Getty Images; p. 11 Robbie Jack/Corbis Entertainment/Getty Images; p. 12 Hiroyuki Ito/Hulton Archive/Getty Images; p. 14 Saul Loeb/AFP/Getty Images; p. 15 (top) Mireya Acierto/Getty Image; p. 16 Julieta Cervantes/The New York Times/Redux Pictures; p. 19 Kevin Mazur/WireImage/Getty Images; p. 20 PR Newswire/AP Images; p. 21 Rabbani and Solimene Photography/Getty Images; back cover, interior pages (curves graphic) Alena Kazlouskaya/Shutterstock.com; interior pages (toe shoes) Jenny Bonner/E+/Getty Images